Polar Corona

by

Caroline Gill

First published 2025 by The Hedgehog Poetry Press,

5 Coppack House, Churchill Avenue, Clevedon. BS21 6QW

www.hedgehogpress.co.uk

Copyright © Caroline Gill 2025

The right of Caroline Gill to be identified as the author of this work has been asserted in accordance with the Copyright, Designs and Patents Act 1988. All rights reserved. No part of this publication may be reproduced, stored in or introduced into a retrieval system, or transmitted in any form, or by any means (electronic, mechanical, photocopying, recording or otherwise) without prior written permissions of the publisher. Any person who does any unauthorised act in relation to this publication may be liable for criminal prosecution and civil claims for damages.

ISBN: 978-1-916830-26-4

Cover image: Adélie penguin jumping between two ice floes © Nick Dale (via iStock). www.nickdalephotography.com

Contents

Preface	7
Crown	9
Flippers	10
Birth	11
Afloat	12
Risk	13
Why?	14
Endurance	15
Acknowledgements	17

For my family

with love

They that go down to the sea in ships...

Psalm 107: 23

PREFACE

Coronavirus (COVID-19) started to appear in our headlines in December 2019 when a global fight for survival began. 'Corona', a word with many associations in the past, will doubtless be inseparably linked to the virus from now on. Without wishing to detract from the gravity of the pandemic, my aim in these pages has been to focus on the word's literal meaning of 'crown'. The crown I have in mind is a Corona of Sonnets; and here I acknowledge John Donne's sonnet cycle, 'La Corona', as an inspiration in terms of the interlinked circular form, although my chosen rhyme scheme is not identical.

Back in 2014 I enrolled on a short course-cum-residency at the Scott Polar Research Institute (SPRI) and Polar Museum in Cambridge, under the auspices of the Poetry School. SPRI holds many artefacts relating to our polar explorers, and I became interested in the art of Dr Edward Adrian Wilson (1872-1912). I find his 1911 image of a lunar corona at Cape Evans (RGS S0021476) particularly arresting. I am also drawn to his penguin sketches. Wilson, the first doctor to reach the South Pole, died with Captain Robert Falcon Scott (1868-1912). The second line of my concluding sonnet acknowledges Sir Ernest Henry Shackleton (1874-1922), who sheltered on Elephant Island in 1916, and was in 'no doubt that Providence' guided his party.

Caroline Gill
Rushmere St Andrew, 2025
www.carolinegillpoetry.com

i
CROWN

In Memoriam Dr Edward Wilson and his companions

As stars illuminate a world of snow,
a painted crown adds lustre to your moon,
which basks in rings of light with dazzling sheen.
You added beauty to the *why?* and *how?*

And yet vast polar tracts remain a void,
a wilderness of wind upon a chart,
a sea of storms to keep the watch alert,
a yard of graves to mark the men who died.

But in their wake a hurricane of words
arrives on wonder-rafts across the years.
The ocean spreads your story as it roars,
and science filters through the voice of bards.

Your lives exuded fortitude and flair;
past aspirations warm the bitter air.

ii

FLIPPERS

Past aspirations warm the bitter air
as hailstones turn in time to shafts of sun.
Spring visitors arrive and rainbows span
the gulf that separates pack ice from fire.

Yet there are wings beneath the Southern Cross
that never flap towards a starry sky;
these flightless penguins waddle to the sea
and weather storms by huddling in a mass.

Their seasons are the opposite to ours,
and there are rookeries in which they breed
among the scattered nests of penguin peers;
a ring of stone suffices for each brood.

The adults aim to see their offspring thrive;
how many incubated eggs are kept alive?

iii

BIRTH

How many incubated eggs are kept alive?
The air is always cold and thieves abound;
when danger strikes, a penguin must defend
its precious clutch from predators above.

Adélie penguins wait, and then one day
an egg-tooth starts to crack an ovoid shell.
Sometimes two chicks are born, but nature will
determine each one's arc of destiny.

The youngsters need to eat to fill out fast;
they peck and jostle for each scrap of food.
Survival instincts may resemble greed,
but soon the time will come to quit the nest.

These flippered birds must set out from their shore;
the pack ice melts as seasons turn once more.

iv
AFLOAT

The pack ice melts as seasons turn once more
and penguins swim beyond their barren coast.
Winds bellow and converge from south and east
as realms of land and ocean start to blur.

The youngsters dive by instinct for their fish;
survival overtakes all other aims
as flippers tackle underwater streams,
where currents pull, creating swirls of wash.

Where do they go, these birds that disappear?
They flip through waves and leave without a trace;
who knows how many juveniles endure
those restless months amid the ocean's ice.

These penguins breed on land, but all agree
Adélies are equipped for life at sea.

v
RISK

Adélies are equipped for life at sea;
their frontal feathers gleam in iceberg white
as feet and flippers help them turn about
and steer a course between the drifts of floe.

These birds chase after silverfish and squid,
but sometimes they fall foul of leopard seals,
who are themselves pursued by killer whales;
in nature, healthy food chains lead to food.

When penguins reach a frozen ledge, they stop
in case a shadow-creature plans to pounce.
An adult takes the plunge; the others glance
and follow as they launch into the deep.

A leopard seal retires; it's hard to snatch
a single penguin from a tight-knit batch.

vi

WHY?

A single penguin from a tight-knit batch
will trust life's course to instinct all the way.
Some humans long to ask the question *why?*
and feel compelled to seek, to find, to watch.

You were those restless souls, unlike your peers
who nodded by the embers, safe at home.
You forged ahead and hoped to fan the flame
of knowledge as you stoked your polar fires.

What was the force within that caused you all
to search for distant lands of snow and rock?
When rodents ran or shimmied up the sail,
did four-pawed shadows lurch around the deck?

Forget the twisting turns of cat and mice;
endurance was the key to locks of ice.

vii

ENDURANCE

In Memoriam Sir Edward Shackleton and his crew

Endurance was the key to locks of ice,
and Providence your guide through storms at sea.
You knew the force of nature could destroy
your efforts in an elephantine race.

The men hid underneath their lifeboat shells,
their bodies weakened by those hostile lands.
You rode the way of whales to help your friends,
defying frostbite, thirst and deadly squalls.

This tale, a hurricane of deed and word,
reflects vast courage in the face of fear.
Your polar insights cannot be ignored;
resolve is tested through the chill of fire.

Endeavours on the ice cause ink to flow
as stars illuminate a world of snow.

ACKNOWLEDGEMENTS

I wish to offer sincere and grateful thanks to Mark Davidson, my publisher at The Hedgehog Poetry Press, who has seen this pamphlet through to publication, having selected *Polar Corona* as the winning entry in his November 2021 Challenge.

I am so thankful for my parents who encouraged me in my literary endeavours from an early age. My father, Timothy Dudley-Smith (d.2024) was known internationally for his hymn texts. He loved to read and recite poems to his three children, Caroline, Sarah and James, as we sat round the fire on winter evenings. My mother, Arlette (d.2007), introduced me to a child's version of Homer's *Odyssey*, which opened my eyes to the spirit of adventure. Immense thanks are due to David Gill, my husband, for supporting me in every possible way and for sharing so fully in my poetic activities.

I owe a huge debt of gratitude to Peter Thabit Jones of The Seventh Quarry Press for believing in my poems and for publishing *Driftwood by Starlight*, my first full collection, in 2021. Sincere thanks are also due to Dr Charlotte Connelly, Susan Richardson and Professor J. R. Watson for their kindness in writing endorsements for the cover of *Polar Corona*.

The sonnets that form this pamphlet have not been published before. They began to take shape after a poetry course-cum-residency at the Scott Polar Research Institute (SPRI) and Polar Museum in Cambridge in 2014. I would like to express my appreciation for the staff at SPRI and for the staff and tutors at the Poetry School; you all worked so hard and with such enthusiasm to lay on this inspiring opportunity. I also wish to thank Alison Chisholm for her input during a poetry correspondence course with The Writers Bureau.

I am grateful for access to the many and varied resources (museum artefacts, archival materials, artworks, publications and websites) that have played a part in the drafting of this text. Perhaps I may mention one or two of the books that I have found particularly informative and helpful.

The Worst Journey in the World, Apsley Cherry-Garrard's 1922 memoir, brought many aspects of Scott's last Antarctic expedition (1910-1913) into focus. It was the perfect complement to *The Last Letters: The British Antarctic Expedition 1910-13*, edited by Heather Lane, Naomi Boneham and Robert D. Smith (SPRI, 2012). I much enjoyed the text and artwork in Edward Wilson's *Birds of the Antarctic*, edited by Brian Roberts (Blandford Press Limited, 1967) and *Edward Wilson's Antarctic Notebooks* (Reardon Publishing, edition of 2011). The latter volume was compiled by David M. Wilson and Christopher J. Wilson, two of Dr Wilson's great nephews, for the centenary of his death in 2012. I must also include *A Tale for Our Generation: An Account of the 'Winter Journey'* (Australian Capital Equity, 2011; Kerry Stokes Collection, Perth) by Edward Wilson and Henry Bowers, with an Introduction by Stephen Martin.

Beau Riffenburgh's *Polar Exploration* (Carlton Books, 2009 and 2010), produced in association with the Royal Geographical Society, offered facsimiles of key documents such as Scott's final diary entry and a letter from Shackleton before he boarded the *Endurance*. I also wish to mention *Last March*, a poetry collection by Kiran Millwood Hargrave (Pindrop Press, 2012), prepared in collaboration with SPRI for the centenary of Captain Scott's final expedition to the South Pole.

www.ingramcontent.com/pod-product-compliance
Lightning Source LLC
Chambersburg PA
CBHW030237100526
44584CB00015BB/1619